CW01192488

# Empty Vessels

BARNARD
PUBLISHING LTD.

Copyright © 2024 Barnard Publishing Ltd

All rights reserved

Disclaimer; This is a work of fiction. Unless otherwise indicated, all the names, characters, businesses, places, events, and incidents in this book are either the product of the author's imagination or used in a fictitious manner. Any resemblance to actual persons, living or dead, or actual events is purely coincidental.

Empty Vessels © Arabella Emms

Cover design © Rachel Lloyd

ISBN 978-1-7395845-7-3

Barnard Publishing Ltd
Wales

barnard.publishing@gmail.com

www.barnardpublishing.co.uk

To everyone who didn't laugh when six year old me
said she wanted to become a writer.

Thank you.

| | |
|---|---|
| the student crying as she smoked her last cigarette | 12 |
| girls tumble out of lifts together | 13 |
| headphones for hades | 14 |
| the lady painting her nails on the 12:49 train | 15 |
| a girl (with blue hair) outside the bar | 16 |
| the middle-aged lady looking sad in the library | 17 |
| cat people | 18 |
| the man whistling down the high street | 19 |
| the man and his dog on the 12:49 train | 20 |
| the girl going to group therapy | 21 |
| spotting her reflection in every surface | 22 |
| about wool and ants | 23 |
| youngsters at protest in 1982 | 24 |
| the student in yellow crocs | 25 |
| the man and the canadian geese following him | 26 |
| i still don't know his name | 27 |
| coffee shop #1 | 28 |
| hand reaching for wall (to help her balance) | 29 |
| drop out | 30 |
| the lady swiping through tinder | 31 |
| in line for good coffee | 32 |
| passing in the rain | 33 |
| insert poem here | 34 |
| shankland reading room | 35 |
| we came across each other at the hospital | 36 |
| homesick | 37 |
| coffee shop #2 | 38 |

| | |
|---|---|
| "i'm a leo, i shouldn't be in this position…" | 39 |
| autumn aesthetics | 40 |
| a saturday shopper | 41 |
| lost girls | 42 |
| optical coherence tomography | 43 |
| i haven't heard off god in a while | 44 |
| mental health walk | 45 |
| crisp packets | 46 |
| victoria | 47 |
| coffee shop #3 | 48 |
| what drew me to you | 49 |
| exam season | 50 |
| she was sitting at the window | 51 |
| the cashier asked me how i was, and i replied: | 52 |
| vessel | 53 |
| artificial city | 54 |
| judging her book by its cover | 55 |
| and for the first time, i missed being a student | 56 |
| christmas cheer | 57 |
| people who come from wildflowers | 58 |
| writing a story backwards | 59 |
| i swear we've met before | 60 |
| start with a handshake | 61 |
| crochet jumpers and striped trousers | 62 |
| text messages become formal language | 63 |
| charity shop bandages | 64 |
| you made me need caffeine | 65 |
| human effort | 66 |
| promotion | 67 |
| when the vase sits empty | 68 |
| odd socks | 69 |
| dead tenacity | 70 |
| ten qualities for strangers | 71 |
| i've changed a few times since then | 72 |
| the things they do to avoid themselves | 73 |
| a hypothetical conversation | 74 |
| the literature student | 75 |
| studying together | 76 |
| the constellation boy on my train | 77 |
| town noticeboard | 78 |
| tourist | 79 |

| | |
|---|---|
| writing in cursive | 80 |
| newly acquired car keys | 81 |
| spritzes of cheap perfume | 82 |
| two flat whites with extra foam | 83 |
| family gathering | 84 |
| food critique | 85 |
| dear eldest daughter | 86 |
| lines of dialogue said by strangers | 87 |
| shadows guard your bedroom | 88 |
| this place | 89 |
| bandaid | 90 |
| february 20th | 91 |
| new address | 92 |
| visiting hours | 93 |
| birthday cake | 94 |
| trust issues | 95 |
| analogue | 96 |
| can't make me think | 97 |
| cafe of fortune | 98 |
| death's-head hawkmoth | 99 |
| peaceful annihilation | 100 |
| shibari tattoos and converse | 101 |
| 6pm girl | 102 |

i've never heard the phrase 'sunny wales' before
but despite all odds the warmth is pouring onto the
pier today
children run the lengths of it
soft chatter of families punctuates the air
the happiest moment of their life
though i can't know this for sure
not unless i asked each person individually
                                *what i'm not about to do*
but i do know is that if you sit there long enough
people turn into strange phantoms you feel compelled
to write poems about.

# the student crying as she smoked her last cigarette

today spent throwing up undigested chunks of identity she claimed at 3am.
expectations
        *slowly*
            lowered like charity shop jeans falling to
                    sticky floors.
she came here to make waves not to live on the dull planes of life that is compromise.
once brazen acts of protest now made at - *respectful* - volumes
this year wore her down like her leggings thinning at the knees
created someone -*something* - she doesn't recognise
far too bitter to be tamed but far too passive to be anything other than harmless.

# girls tumble out of lifts together

alliteration laced between their outfits
and rudimentary rhymes leaving their lips.
ugly laughter sloshes around with sounds,
they sculpt tonight with their own bare hands
                              and name it *history*.
faces and names pass them with a shadow's swiftness
lost to their slow forming descriptions as the
steady rising dawn – or setting sun – splashes
on the patchwork pavements beneath their feet.
a soft april light allowing them a second bloom.

# headphones for hades

unwritten thoughts drowned out by song
and the unrivalled pressure to be seen as strong.
when asked which is more important, he simply points

>to a roadmap half discovered,
>to moments where being in the spotlight stings his eyes,
>and even a hint of attention feels like a crowded room.

recharged by a lack of silence
but happy in places unseen
there's a pause as he thinks back
to the lonely age of eighteen.
counting the beats between breaths
the next album is played
waiting for the song that will call for persephone
where they'll dance till they become unmade.

# the lady painting her nails on the 12:49 train

*"come home for christmas"*
wary conversation held between estranged mother
       and daughter.
unfocused voices strained through mobile phone.
thoughts of one cigarette
       turns to glasses of wine.
            *another and another.*
faded moment of self-pity rising.
the journey back was too long.
       *too short,*
       *a delay would have been nice.*
hour by hour tracks pass under carriage,
leaving doubtful footsteps in her mind,
picturing glimpses of disapproving faces as she opens
the front door.
pale blue nails - the only thing wearing down the
resemblance between her
and everyone else inside.

# a girl (with blue hair) outside the bar

hand me down denim jacket worn on the days
when she needed to feel the strength
of those before her.
woven fabric defends from elements
her skin porous as topsoil.
worms make up veins
wriggle to heartbeat.
her roots should touch the ground
but she crafted them into two french braids.
ends exposed to air
grasping for stability in the space of a breeze.
just like how she looks for stability in drunken nights
and aquamarine eyeshadow worn to feel pretty.
in these moments where hollow boned hands grab her waist,
she wishes she could settle her soul in something.
something that wasn't a fraying denim jacket
and the red plastic cup a stranger handed to her
with a suggestive smile.

# the middle-aged lady looking sad in the library

she finds solace among the stories
where the gold embossing is worn down
lost to eager hands reaching for knowledge
lines around her eyes
embedded deep in skin
broken strokes tell tales written by time
in these moments escape is found
amongst the spines wrapped in canvas and leather
stained by oily fingers of a hundred strangers
head buried in work
*this is a distraction*
*an attempt to stop the*
*bleeding*
using torn out pages as bandages
to stop the ink seeping out of her chest

# cat people

longing for the saran wrapped sandwiches your dad
used to make you for lunch.
he never lied to you about what you did and didn't
have.
when everyone else had all the shades of the rainbow
and delicate pastels
you had primary colours
sturdy and reliable,
one-dimensional until you know how to mix them
that's what your dad would say.
on the bus journey home, you'd hope to exchange your
good karma for a fogged-up window seat.
waiting to get away from school girls
and boys with stupid hair.
to return home and be half welcomed by the local stray
you adopted last summer.
now a spoiled little thing
setting you on the path to becoming the crazy cat lady,
such a label you have no intention of shaking.
your ribs crack with the weight of familiarity
between you and your tender gran
        a cat person too.
a lady who always noticed the blush on your cheeks
as your crush passed you by.

# the man whistling down the high street

he is familiar,
a constant in this elastic city
his residence wherever he laid his hat that day.
browsing the faces of passers-by
sorting through those who demand attention
that sound.
        that sound etched into minds.
                a mewl that wandered down the high
            street.

# the man and his dog on the 12:49 train

he never asked me to understand,
so i never questioned.
self-editing his life story
twisting truths with metaphors,
trying to distinguish him from me
train journey shared.
his dog sleeping in the walkway,
to let the other passengers know he was there.

# the girl going to group therapy

i never realised there was an art to breaking
my technique improving
collecting dog-ends of thoughts fused with
rituals
compulsions
i ask this out right
how much longer do i need to repeat these
words
    words
        words create pamphlets to give to
strangers
an insight into a confessional that
    should
have been kept private

but i suppose it is    unnatural
to keep a masterpiece hidden behind a curtain

# spotting her reflection in every surface

world spiralling like orange peel
still unsure how to unravel without splitting
hazy mind bursting with fragrance as the pulp tears
a sore heart left the mottling colour of winter flu
remembering how his shampoo smelt better on her
night spent saving the texts they sent
borrowed maps to the other's core
plotted during a time he thought he knew a feeling
an easy evening watching silent films
frustration smothered by fulfilment
as she rests her head in his lap

# about wool and ants

i don't know who lives in that body,
their life withheld from me.
conversations with another stranger
carried across the street.
something of importance is being said,
though i'm frankly unsure what.
they could save me a lot of time guessing
if only they turned around. turned towards
me. towards the bench adorned with bird shit
i uncomfortably sit on.
i can see their pain in the wool they wear,
woven in the roving.
as i sit deeper into my seat
i wish that the ants next to me
could murmur into their ear
                  to just *let go*.

# youngsters at protest in 1982

peculiar choice of word when they're clearly children
three sit, each a daffodil in hand
traces of green nuances in its fragrance
i know to exist because it'll be the same today
as it was back then.
only history bringing a contrast to the image before me
coats dented from the time sitting on the ground
i suspect if it were in colour i'd find familiarity in the
redness in their faces
as mine often is when i get back home
but i can't read myself in this picture
yet i know we've been here before
not me personally
but the wider we.

# the student in yellow crocs

some parts were beautiful.
nestled in artisan coffeehouse,
writing poems based on fellow coffee shop girls.

she was an adult of course.
    *a young adult admittedly.*
still needing guidance for the little things,
    the odd reminder from her mother not to leave
    damp clothes in the washing machine,
    that four-day old pizza wasn't safe to eat,
    the nudge off professors not to leave her
    assignments too late.

her focus spent on laptop screen writing frantic emails to her tutor.
subject line:   *enquiry about essay*
        *question about the essay*
        *essay due soon*
        *what am I mean to be doing?*
        *i'm freaking out about this essay*
        *help!!*
deep sigh absorbed by ambient noise waiting for response.
these weren't steady times for her
her happy place – university,
where all debts were waiting to be paid.

# the man and the canadian geese following him

water and gunk - the depths of december
webbed feet with secrets to share
    one says
        *"i prefer the days he brings the bread"*
    the other replies
        *"fingers are better"*
today he brought nothing
wanting to be alone - no care for their conversations
the swans don't engage in such talk
he'll go see them instead

# i still don't know his name

i met him at the stone circle
before the cherry blossoms were planted
ornamental pink buds sprouting from young bark
wind or shine he would be at his bench
the grass changing from mundane green
to coarse and dead under his feet

on some of my walks i stray from the path
looking to rest in the slowness
leaning on a torso of bark
where time speaks to the roots, curling knots
reaching towards fellow lean-to trees
i see none of this, its motion hidden
i too feel hidden here

but weaving through the foliage,
the man's full body laugh always makes it to me.

we've exchanged many pleasantries through the years
a constant among the uncertainty
his smile taking up far too little room
and now i start to worry as i prepare to come home
that he will remain the man whose name i never
knew.

# coffee shop #1

conversation dances in the space between half-held hands.
remembering back to that lunch
when he asked elderly ladies which type of flowers to buy.
learning that they're cheaper when it rains.
this evening to be spent pretending they're artists.
the words they whisper to be carried across telephone lines of
paper cups and string.
there's plenty of time tomorrow, for the things unsaid today.

# hand reaching for wall (to help her balance)

*where she goes, i do not know*
perhaps picturing a panorama of her future
or wondering how hearing *i love you* will feel in her ear
*the why is no matter to me*
noticing how the sleeve of her jumper resembles my own
picked apart by nerves and chipped nail polish
there are hundreds of people in this city with a reflection of each other in their eyes
*and i'm beginning to wonder if i'm one of them*

# drop out

you thought the days of mumbling answers under your breath were over,
yet your eyes pretend to focus on the professor at the front.
a shop set up in their throat,
just to charge you to hear the words that come out of it.
*naturally, no refunds are allowed.*
not even next week,
where memories will be tested and even the echoes are inspected.
but here you sit, by your own choice,
each assignment becomes a voicemail in the back of your mind
                         *and the phone just won't stop ringing.*

# the lady swiping through tinder

backpack straps curled around converse,
loose laces reaching to collect dust bunnies under the seat.
in this suffocating box strangers sit stiffly
waiting - *no, hoping* - to be anything but a mild annoyance to those around,
like the plump pigeons on the high street.
they've been around so long we've tuned out their coos
only making themselves known when you feed them scraps
regretting it the moment they flock.
*i know a thing or two about regret*
but i don't have the time to deconstruct life further just now.
she's lost to her phone and i'm getting off at the next stop.

# in line for good coffee

it's tuesday
brooding over a laptop and library books – line
between his eyes
it's only tuesday
there's something waiting to happen – but she's
forgotten what it is
forgotten till she occupies the space next to him
pleasantries back on the mind
a pleasurable anxiety forming
little things need to be established in this meeting
            she likes soft cover notebooks
            he doesn't like ice in his drinks
            they both like music from the 2010s
he listens as she reads and talks when she speaks
one of them is writing the first draft of their story on
the backs of postcards and second class stamps
      *i'll let you guess who*
it's the same thing as bringing three water bottles to a
lecture because you know water evaporates
as a name is called out and order collected
the other is picturing an easy night
where they get id'd for buying energy drinks and
strawberry laces together

## passing in the rain

everything sounds more beautiful in the rain
but the church bells are lost to ears lent out to a
polyester hood
curls peeking from under it
greedily taking water into fattening strands

all the weather rhymes here
to the point where she opened her mouth and
almost said something
*almost*
on her journey home she keeps away from the edges of
the living pavement
foliage sprouting through glistening cracks
how accurately can we predict the rain?
waiting for it to pool into cupped hands
left shaking in wet clothes
waterproofs peeling open like lilies

# insert poem here

i won't let you be a blank page
but you had one of those stories i couldn't share.
so i kept you as scribbles and half written words,
a scrap of paper hidden in my pocket.
when i washed my jeans i forgot where you were.
mulch in my hand – perhaps it was for the best for i
can't be tempted to write.
so my dear reader, please do me a favour and insert a
poem here
>
> *because i don't have one.*

# shankland reading room

i met a stranger through the booklice
her scent of wood stain and musk
home - a shelf turned to puzzle
now missing a piece.

time had not been kind
spine warped though age
watching others walk by
not giving her their gaze.

my priorities are different now
essay due in hours
no time to make her acquaintance.
but i'm certain when i collapse into her story,
i'll never fall again.

# we came across each other at the hospital

thoughts forming in poorly constructed sentences
mouth opened, vomiting rivers of white noise that
could bounce off valley walls
> on the outside it could have been mistaken for rage
>
> on the outside it could have been mistaken for pain
>
> on the outside mistake it as anything other than what it was

specific modules of her brain misfiring
a failed conversation between chemicals and neurons
currents reverberating off the curvatures
> *a neuro form of genesis*

bringing the human back to a sterile, clinical diagnosis

# homesick

last night spent sleeping on a stomach of 49p ramen
at home there's comfort food on the stove and nanna's bread in the pantry
longing to be in his childhood room again
where the bedding has bobbled, and mattress springs feel like a rock.
right now he could have rocks in his stomach – full of nerves
> *he refuses to acknowledge any of this*
> *whatever this is*
taking the taxi home is like choosing violence when arguing with a toddler
it's only gratifying when you're feeling insecure
> *what he's not i'm sure*
but there's £7 in his account and shrapnel of pennies in his pocket
his dad would say there's a lesson in that
*somewhere.*

# coffee shop #2

in class someone said that only love poems contain people
if that were the case i'd start this poem with
    'i saw you when no one else did.'
but that's not true, the barista knows you by name.
in my head you are the person who rushes to the door
and yet, today
you sip your coffee four tables across from me.

you remind me of me
    solidifying that this is not a love poem.
in fact, i'm proud to say i've never written one despite having my own muse.
i will admit though, i don't know what i'm looking for in you.
chewing your hoodie strings - coffee long forgotten
fibre is better than flesh
the scars on the inside of my cheeks can testify.

you gather here like me
like broken things
breathing a collective sigh of relief when we slip on by unnoticed.

## "i'm a leo, i shouldn't be in this position…"


if she wrote a novel people wouldn't be able to identify with the characters,
or at least that's what she told the lady across the table.
a friend turning stranger.
someone she hoped could run a brush through her tangles of pain,
soothe her and show her the correct shelf to store her rage.
her last therapist reported her *but i wasn't meant to hear that.*
      switch to the other side of the table
where the silence is held a little too long,
shoulders sink and arms reaches for bag
"i need to go to the toilet."
*i saw her sneak out the other door but i wasn't supposed to.*

## autumn aesthetics

she was the type of person you thought you saw in a crowd.
layered cable knit tights and mustard socks
choked on october
where the comfort of her whole being can be found among the fallen leaves
soon to be snagged by frost.

there's always one we don't like, but it wasn't her.
no, she was the sort to sweep around in the wind.
and then, at that moment you realise
just how insulated you are
from her
from burning pain and sobs of envy
waiting for a moment of ugliness to feed your imperfect desires
to prove to your mind that 'at least it was expected'
then the seasons change
and autumn is left behind.

# a saturday shopper

wandering through the public with disinterest
a young peacock passes her by
the street becomes less crowded
falling in line with every other courtyard flower
waiting for the gardener to notice her

a dragonfly's hind legs bow her stem with the weight of its landing
local honey bees lap up every petal
sunlight is lost to the branches of neighbouring trees
taking her world and shoving it into a sentence

she almost recognises the place that she's in
familiarity waiting to be pushed out
vanished by any ceremony she likes
break fish bones and burn them
mix the ashes with honey till the embers carry their smell into the air
drift away into nothingness
*what a time to be alive.*

# lost girls

louise holds daffodil bulbs in her pocket
each one a dream to grow.
petals from her mother's daisy lives in a locket,
her sister's dead leaves lost in the snow.

martha rips her jeans for fun,
frayed blue like the curls of her hair.
her denim jacket bleached by the sun,
the turmoil in her heart laid bare.

and anne weaves feathers into french braids,
hoping one day she'll learn to fly.
escape the pressure of future and grades,
she locks her bedroom door to cry.

## optical coherence tomography

her eyes were like trees
not in the poetic sense
more that the back of them were full of branches
and when i say that
i mean when i looked behind them
i could see the roots of her inner thoughts
capillaries swarming her optic disk
pulsing in the unknowing
the space of this moment and the rest of her life
where i knew the bad news before she did

# i haven't heard off god in a while

big man in the sky stays silent.
so, i ride my bike off the church walls.
or at least i did in a daydream.
there's still a part of me that wishes i'd really done it.
during my descent off a wall a sheet of paper would fly
out my pocket.
paper in air,
white wings flapping,
take me away.
there's a lady in the graveyard that will talk to me
when god is silent.
each day she's by a new resting place.
her back curved like a broken bridge,
frail yet permanent as if she came from the headstones
herself.

the mice she feeds whisper useless magic
to one another.
an army of pink feet,
an unsettling repeating pattern of behaviour.
the longer i spend with her the louder the
subconscious warnings are.

at night, she sits under the only elder tree for miles,
ethereal green cover,
viridescent leaves sprout from decaying ground.
the universe is woven between the roots.
pull away the soil to find a blanket of life,
i'll be honest with you, it's disappointing.
but i can't write about this anymore,
because i haven't heard off god in a while,
and i'm starting to worry he's not there.

## mental health walk


there's zero chance this walk is relaxing
not according to the o.e.d definition
each step diluting the hellish kind of rage only youth could create
the sort where you establish yourself in the centre of a hurricane and 'forget'
to ask your conciseness how it really feels about it

there's no gate at the park she's in
no way for her to know if she's in or out of it - ruining her internal commentary
just like when doctors advise her against categorising her moods into lipstick colours
recommending a model of thinking that opens her up to the kind of analysis
that shrinks her lungs and takes a jackhammer to her spleen

## crisp packets

i'd just got my hearing aids when i sat in front of you on the train     i don't recall seeing your face or who you were but you had a bag of crisps     your loud, loud bag of crisps

every time you touched it, it was as if you'd reached into me, grabbed my spine and scraped your gnarly fingers down my bones     down every vertebrae dry nails scratched

i assumed the ordeal was over till you reached your hand to your mouth     that disgusting, wet, saliva filled mouth     grotesque sucking on fingers followed

who puts their fingers in their mouth on a train? where the dandruff of the person before you is now embedded in your hair     the grease of a forehead is smeared on the window after someone fell asleep against it - an unintentional prism refracting light in all the wrong ways

yet there you were, globs of saliva now running down your fingers     i wanted to say how disgusting you were     wanted you to be rude to me if i turned around and confronted you     give me a reason to justify my dislike towards you     but you were just eating your lunch and i was just overwhelmed hearing the world clearly for the first time in too long.

to the person behind me on the 10:05 train to wolverhampton, i'm sorry i glared daggers at the seat in front of me, pretending it was your head.

*Arabella Emms*

## victoria

there's a girl who wears roller-skates on the street i live
setting off from home with slow pushes
wheel tracks contorting lines – moving in and out like breath
cheeks flushed – crafted by the bloom of april flowers and wind
she rides smiling with spearmint lips
there are thousands of words in existence and somehow
i can't find the right ones to describe how her life differs from mine
*but just know it does.*

# coffee shop #3

the slaps of cards on the table are lost
to coffee shop sounds. just as the slow drag of
my page is left unheard as i near the end of
this chapter.

crumbs stick to fingers, stick to the winning hand.
condensation from my glass cools my fingers
then waters the pages of my book. we're all hiding
from the heat in here.
matching iced drinks.
short shorts and sunburnt knees.

i'm glad i'm not the only one who's learning to switch off.
briefly, i ponder if i should ask to join in.
he's teaching her how to play.
she's leaning on her hands and smiling when he's not looking.

there's a rhythm in our slowness,
this lazy sunday,
where the music plays in the background
and heat drags along the pavement.

## what drew me to you

you said thank you to the receptionist
even though they messed up your booking,
pulled out a book instead of a phone
the tyrian purple cover caught my eye
i'd never seen that title before.

you had ginger hair and i'd always wanted that
at school i'd tell my friends as a baby i had red hair too
        but it all grew out.
or swear it was auburn in the sun,
ignoring the evening before
where i covered it in henna dye wearing my california t-shirt
an unintentional sunset stained onto my nails.

one of the pins on your bag had slipped upside down
and i overheard that you'd just moved house
it made me think of when i'd turn an empty box into a time machine
markers stain small fingers
smile held for literal hours

you made me realise i wanted to start opening up boxes of memories
i'd tried so hard to keep closed.

*Empty Vessels*

## exam season

she draws flowers on the corner of her page,
knotted thoughts.
hands run along paper expecting to feel leaves coated
in morning dew.
the cold stings her throat.
maybe if she breathes it long enough the daisies will
grow in her voice,
their fibrous roots reach deep into her lungs,
a tap root wraps too tight on an exhale.
what's wrong with breathing dirt and dead leaves?
the forest in her core rots with the promise of a
beautiful unfolding,
winter has passed, she will appear once more.
but like flowers on a page she will never bloom.
petals made of ink never grow.
so she draws flowers on the corner of her page.

# she was sitting at the window

leant over lamp lit desk,
it's 2 am
lost in parchment paper, poetry and caffeine
wishing       for      one         more
night.
let me show you the call of monsters lost in violins,
how the dark isn't as scary as the light.
telling each other ghost stories
as you plant yourself next to me.

i will walk you through the woods in your back garden
wearing wildflowers as perfume.
we'll ride on stolen bicycles as you work out the exact shade of my hair,
the right word to describe how my hand looks next to yours.

50p raspberry sweets turn our tongues blue
and energy drinks spill on hand-me-down denim.
nicotine and menthol hang over a driftwood fire in late october.
nostalgia from a time you never lived.
but it's 2 am
and i wonder if i will feel it when you write me into a sunrise.

# the cashier asked me how i was, and i replied:

i started a new job and it's going really well.
but sometimes i still feel sick when i wake up in the morning.
i see hundreds of people a day yet i see myself in every frown.
i'm searching for someone else to word my discomfort because i can't accept a smile was because of me.
my bones fuse to flesh, but not literally.
so when the doctor asks me to rate my pain on a scale to 1 to 10, i say 7.

> *i'm fine thanks. you?*

# vessel

here once more
feeling the sun press my side
a comforting hand steadying me
its light travelling through me
    *through my transparency*
foot loosely tracing uneven flooring
left wondering how many versions of me
    *the cookie cutter student*
    *optimistic young adult*
have occupied this seat this year
taking fantastic notes of passers-by
slow drips of life

today my hands hold my head
coffee cup on borrowed books
gathering stains on chipped ceramic
its bottom indenting the cover below
    *i pay it no mind*
thoughts instead occupied past the window
my wandering eyes
        drowning
in the lives i see

## artificial city

i fear the day will come where gentleness is forgotten.
cut out my tongue for not joining in with the anger.
why are the kind punished as if they did something wrong?

i choose not to use my voice.
soft speech mocked; i will be eaten if i utter a word.
it's like they know we are dangerous when free.

i want to stay innocent at any cost.
so, i hide under a blanket of poems and learn to dance to a rhyme.
a slight disruption of the air is the only indicator i'm alive.

## judging her book by its cover

under the linen voices gather
a hushed mutiny taking place
100-watt light bulbs strung across the room,
leaving a hidden code for those who know.

an anaemic girl walks along the hall,
her thoughts made up of disregarded lines from the
poets that came before.
rags and ribbons laced across broken ribs
under the linen voices gather
a hushed mutiny taking place

# and for the first time, i missed being a student

i say it was my bench she was sitting on,
but we all know seats are fair game.
what i mean is that it was my seat,
my seat to be absorbed into the silence on a still winters day,
or to be lost to birdsong turn summer.
my place to watch strangers pass me by and turn them into poems.
my safe place to close my eyes and just be,

it wasn't just that she was taking my seat
but she was taking my place too.
sat crossed legged, engrossed in a book.
heck, i'd read that very book on that bench.
her eco friendly flask balanced on the slats,
i was half tempted to ask about its contents.
hazarding a guess that it'd be the same
as the 50p coffee sachets i used to use,

now i sit across, feet aching from work,
drifting since getting my degree.
hoping to find purpose in the people that i see.
left daydreaming about spring evenings
and how fulfilled i thought i'd be
      when i no longer called myself a student.

## christmas cheer

peppermint snaps across her wrist,
she bleeds along lines of green and red.
spilled hot chocolate burns exposed skin.
a cosy night turns into a nightmare,
the doors are locked but she's not safe.
vanilla candles burn on the bookshelf,
the smell chokes her.
paper cuts on her hands from wrapping her memories
away.

# people who come from wildflowers

lost amongst blades of grass,
thoughts sway with spring winds.
damp earth settles under beat up trainers,
scuffs on the rubber tell more tales than the trees
could ever share.
two lovers hands entwine.
she is the sun.
he wears a flower crown to show her glory.
                        how precious are those born
                        amongst the wildflowers.

## writing a story backwards

burnt tongue on another and she's lost all sense of taste.
fingers become liars as they type on the screen,
looking for any excuse to be in his company.
and if he can't say yes?
well, there's still hope for an answer anyway.

# i swear we've met before

we have the same comfort hoodie - at least that's what mine is used for
used on the days where heart crawls up oesophagus scared of when someone gets to know you and claims false advertising
you know, a cherry blossom falls at five centimetres per second
meaning i could walk across the room and say hello before 50 of them reach the ground

but i won't

## start with a handshake

if this month lasted more than a year
and the government introduced boredom tax
you'd still be grateful
that you're not some middle manager with limping dreams

and if you are then pick yourself up off the floor
smile with your eyes for it is courteous to do so
you want the poets to notice you when you walk into the room
don't hang yourself with your own dry tongue
remember, even cats have etiquette

## crochet jumpers and striped trousers

they say getting a real job is safer than creating art
but that's a matter of perspective
> when picking flowers is a slasher horror for the plants
> but an act of decoration for you

so whilst the philosophers and parents decide what counts as real
you hide behind your self imposed glass mountain
> where country music plays on the radio
> > and you wrestle with your socially acceptable disorder known as discipline.

# text messages become formal language

words once spoken close to the ear become misheard whispers.
somewhere along the line friends became background actors,
leaving you understanding why a willow might weep.
realising no one could hurt you as much as you hurt yourself.
trapped in the three dimensional form that is your life,
some ornate cage keeping you on display as one big cosmic joke.
it is of no matter though,
for you have found your place on the oceans of apathy.

i'm sure your life is beautiful, but i'm glad it's not mine.

# charity shop bandages

we know lots of stories yet
you never seem to know the ones i know
from what you've told me of yours it's left me wondering
        wondering if you're waiting
for nerve endings to die
or to become woven into a tapestry.
a creation so haunting
        it leaves the master craftsman tossing in his sleep.

i guess what i'm trying to say is,
when it stops hurting
        please don't be proud of it.

## you made me need caffeine

you think your existence is shading in someone elses sketchbook
mistaking tablecloths for a map of your life
finding direction in the crumbs     imaginary landmarks
when your name is called half the room turn their heads
     yet yours doesn't move
locked in an attempt to unravel the dark laces that bind you,
     that comfort you
a corset hugging, strangling your left lung
oh beautiful body cavity between rib cage

     nevermind your excuses
you can't sail a stationary ship
but a vessel made of broken parts?
     that can go anywhere

*shame you haven't learned that yet*

# human effort

i pictured you having the power of a universe in your exhale
that you know the polite thing would be to let yourself be forgotten
        but you won't
because you know there's only a finite amount of times you can be knocked down.

        and to stay down would be to leave your story incomplete
        words left scattered on the back of receipts yet to be translated

so carry on brushing your teeth with kids toothpaste
and requesting ice with your drinks
because it's rare to be someone who knows water can flow uphill,
and it's even rarer to be someone who tries

## promotion

back turned to victorian nightgown walls
where sour statements fall from blank paper people

in an hour's time when bones threaten to collapse
eyes will search for plastic cups filled with headache remedy
only then will you join in with the applause and

quietly lie to yourself
that the money was worth it

## when the vase sits empty

you tended to the water and not the plants
your pupils drank in the realisation that spring day
noticed how the lilies were no trouble
and the dianthus took little space to grow
but you cracked and creaked like dried wood
making yourself as welcome as japanese knotweed
needing to be destroyed by fire

the root rot had setted in
so you hoped to find peace in weed killer
letting the foliage take your place
for flowers know how to commit themself
to being one thing

# odd socks

one could say she's embracing a life that bends
claiming mismatched socks are a work of art
a way to tell her apart from everyone else who claims
to be unique
you could spin this into a tale
that mismatched feet encompasses a soul that's wild
and free

but i'll hazard a guess she doesn't even realise
the dots and stripes on each foot

that she was running late this morning
hit snooze one too many times
dreading the thought of another day working 9-5

# dead tenacity

if i had to guess i'd say he's the type to greet fate a little drunk
would say a £3 meal deal is feasting like a king
and about 17 minutes after midnight
is when he lies awake
holding out bribed to street lights
asking them to turn into stars.

## ten qualities for strangers

some speak softly and make it their whole personality
others use books to better themselves
i know one who decorated their room with their spines.

one i met befriends all as a way to see the world
        they can't leave the house much.

loss of a loved one is the most painful element oneself
i've seen

on the other hand, quiet drunk is always fun to be
around
        they'll tell you random facts
                and giggle at naked statues when
            visiting        the museum
when they're sad they put hot sauce on their food
and smile when their sibling gives them a segment of
orange
        one of them has something the other wants
                as siblings always do

# i've changed a few times since then

there's a whispering sound coming from their pocket
some soft spoken soul looking for a permanent state of self
who understands the perspective of the deer in the headlights at 2am
and won't turn something like selfishness into a weapon
they say they're iron and they'll forge themselves

how wonderful it must be to be young
and so willing to get yourself killed

## the things they do to avoid themselves

the girl across from me recovers her small attitude
the lady to my right pulls out magazine clippings from her bag
leaning into envious space
desperation as clear as the gossip we shared as children
under the faint glow of led candles and discount fairy lights
dropping tomato pasta on sleeping bags
as we talked about the friend that isn't there

# a hypothetical conversation

there's a plea dancing on their lips
no words make a sound but we can hear all attempts
at deception
the desire to be struck by disaster
just to avoid looking to another's eyes
it's invasive and they'll unravel
like the impending awareness of feeling their heart
beat when no one wants it to.

## the literature student

the future is coming too fast
an amalgamation of gorgeous chaos
some unfair, wonderful things
there's no word in the english language for it

knowledge of who they were this morning
they won't be the same when they rest tonight
you could say they're looking for symbolism in the search party
as the person they seek is shouting out the night sky name.

## studying together

when existing is too much
when they've been walking a road where no flowers grow
they'll understand the call to live
to stop seeing the world from someone else's point of view
to stop pondering the most beautiful questions
and start asking them instead

## the constellation boy on my train

thoughts chase themselves down a passing hill
there's a book half opened on his bouncing knee
the tap of his shoe disembodied from dissociating mind
engine sounds mix with train tracks passing under
and the lights in windows create incomplete mosaics of others lives

this is the type of human playground i can get behind
they type where i watch and he says nothing
already knowing i'm fluent in awkward silence.

# town noticeboard

tucked away in a haphazard corner disregarded paper created a mural
some arduous picture of complicated information
aiding in the communal inability to recall things

posters claim they're only mean to people who deserve
    it
the villain will always be evil if the hero wrote the story
such an important matter passed over in silence as the next generation
loses themselves to sips of coffee and trying to make everyone happy

# tourist

finding herself unfurling in the rhythm of a crowd
where human tales line the air and
refuge is found in streaming trails
hours pass and sunlight slips through the glass
she starts to gather the parts of her lost to life's demands
cherishing every word laced with depth
the postcards she collects remain empty
destined to be bolted onto bedroom walls

# writing in cursive

unsure of what to do with your hands
anything is better than clawing at mottled skin
painting with shades of bruises

stuff your tight knuckled fists into trouser pockets
chew the inside of your gum to strips of meat
       gasp of breath
          an acceptance
              of the loss soon to arrive
as you prepare yourself to take your foot
     *ankle exposed and all*
and place it on the rung
of the glass ladder you
dreamt about last summer

# newly acquired car keys

whilst you love this place you don't
understand why you
                      love this moment
carrying yourself, socks and shoes in hand
as you dance your way through second hand smoke
        inhaling breath into a body
            with no safe haven
callous feet step over champagne rocks     grains
of sand make way between teeth
        reminding yourself of the impracticability
of a smile

# spritzes of cheap perfume

autumn coats you in a damp second skin
as the rain changes time
you need two layers of socks when
        left unsupervised with your thoughts

once again trying to lose yourself to
the same body of water that turns beer bottles into
seaglass

the discovery that you're apart of gravity, dust mites
and stolen pint glasses
        you know only to take the branded ones
you know to take the bus home
        filled with half awake passengers and a driver
that smiles at your exit

## two flat whites with extra foam

i'd hazard a guess he
laughs when he burns
his garlic bread and that
an extra sachet of sugar
will be added to his
drink
he's nervous
to remember
the early days
the easy day
it's easier to carve
thoughts into chalk
then to talk them through
with a friend
instead they sit trying
to find meaning in spirals
of fence posts with the
tagline of art
artificial streams of dopamine
sitting on the balcony
turning people into ants
then humans again

# family gathering

you turn plant pots into wine pitchers
vandalising love letters of tangled stems as
vermont petals drift under the bookshelf
loaded shelves support delicious tales
like the shawl you wear
smuggled from paris
by your grandmother's once youthful hands
                           *the landline rings*
fruit twist still lingers on lips
you've practised sarcasm by writing
on the backs of hands
and said hello 320 times in
the mirror     yet the conversation to be had
is far too important to be
started by pleasantries and
hopeful smiles no one can see

## food critique

there were raisins in my cake
and the lady at the counter laughed when i called
them dead flies

i've learned that i rattle coffee shop owners
i order my food and start writing in my notebook
i tell them i'm a poet, nothing more, nothing else
perhaps to them it's easier to believe someone is here
to judge
then to sit alone

left alone with every version of oneself
i draw out every sip of my blood orange iced tea
as i name every city pigeon i have the privilege of
meeting

i've learned i have to eat those pesky dead flies

## dear eldest daughter

building yourself a second hand house of cards
queen of hearts- owners or everyone's but your own
playing the joker at every turn
performance and person merge
till its 4am where blues music and wine made from concentrate
teach you there's no such thing as self love.

# lines of dialogue said by strangers

little black door with the swinging bell at the top
splinters    on the lips    muscles screwed tight
sitting cross legged on the kitchen counter
slicing shin bones    catching light from LED bulbs
i write my prayers down on    brown paper bags
waiting
at the botanical garden

## shadows guard your bedroom

eavesdropping melodies through second story floorboards
the nocturnals play soft piano keys on the winter solstice
songs contort to their composer and you wish you could do the same
wishing you could trust yourself like you do your spleen
      even though you don't know what it does
      you just know you have one and it   *works*
when you try to sing along to song that rise through the floor
lose chalk fills your mouth
people tell you that your pupils are made out of new moons
they haven't figured out that the mind behind them is eclipsed

# this place

held as dear as jewellery collected from the gaps of
train seats and nightclub bathrooms
we're waiting for this city to behave
waiting for it's ghosts to leave our lungs
> *go pollute somewhere else*
> *go fester somewhere else*
> *go die somewhere else*

strong faces hold pinpoint stare and minds rot along
the street
bearing teeth and dying eyes
you know it's bad when the saints on church walls
have turned their backs

# bandaid

papercuts from poetry covers where i play make belief with strangers
a vein is opened each time i want to talk to you
in those lilac washed night
        tangles of my hair spell out love letters on my shower wall
i'll use the the lipgloss 'borrowed' from my friend and steal
        the right kind of words form telephone cords

 all this,
        all this just so i can carry a touch
that makes the weight of my patchwork skin bearable.

# february 20th

made up of moth balls and table salt
mirroring the ghosts that pass each night
graveyard apparitions held you during heartbreak
you held yourself as pain collected in every pathway
that required oxygen
you're becoming increasingly found each day,
a car crash kid     emotional whiplash and lasting
scars
now an adult checking blindspots in reflections

# new address

the consequences of your actions - a souvenir placed on your windowsill
sat proudly next to gifted succulents, bobby pins and lose change
in this room outside conversations weave themselves into strands of hair
lodged in the brush thrown carelessly on your desk
here boots with creased leather half hide under your bed will walk further than your perceived future
in these yellow hour mornings you'll make plans to leave this
unvisitable, unspeakable place

## visiting hours

copper laced blood wearing silver jewellery and plastic tubes
black chasm for a frontal lobe,
pain has you curling in an infirmary
thinking of infinity
left aching for boring moments and the taste
of beige summers
where you dodge cracks in pavements
and pick at dirt under pale mauve nails

# birthday cake

bleach surfaces then hair
fumes fill birthday balloon lungs as you welcome your thirties
fingertips stagger across phone screen, helping you tread water
till sunset
where you'll carve midnight drenched quotes into tired ivory bones
walking into the wake of a thousand more tomorrow, knowing that
the world doesn't end this year

## trust issues

and you asked me to watch you stuff - you'll be gone ten minutes. you asked me
not the seven other people around us. you asked me, the damp dynamite girl with
a chasm in my throat, the one contemplating if cursed vinyl records could still play church hymns.
you asked me and your back was turned before i even saw your face. you put a lot of trust in someone who doesn't trust themselves.

# analogue

in one day there's over 7 billion sunsets
you can't convince me that we're all seeing the same one
you seem to find yours mid winter in vapour clouds
passing under streetlights as you walk home
ritualistic checking of the mirror to check that it's safe
the lamp posts turn into halos in your departure

## can't make me think

sunlight delivering contrast to tattooed skin
walking museum of fine art
the sole keeper of recurring daydreams and half arsed
conspiracy theories
trusting in panic and babble

## cafe of fortune

complain about the wooden spoon given to you
splinters in drink
splinters in tongue halting your small suggestion to
the question proposed
make no peace offering nor grasp for forgiveness
syrup on the corner of mauve lips
sweet invitation to delirium as you compare polaroids
taken today
look at you, you solo hymn, you offering of solitude
collecting mementos of the moments you broke your
isolation.

## death's-head hawkmoth

dazzled by headlights as you wonder home
misplaced pity for creatures who fly towards the light
resisting the urge to become lost in the bleeding ink
sky
hopelessly wishing the atmosphere would fracture
just so you could brag about seeing what's on the
other side

## peaceful annihilation

big crash, break glass you clever, clever animal
head thrown sideways as your visible heartbeat calls to the sky
ask me to spill all my secrets then demand something more
cinnamon candles and spearmint gum - threads of memories of you
memories of nights you turned wine glasses into telescopes
searching for the recommended dose of serotonin
wearing rings on your fingers that would make saturn jealous

# shibari tattoos and converse

the most important pawn on your board is the one you sacrifice
i mean, its got a purpose and that's important right?
it's important in the same way therapists use outrageously long silences
a way to 'encourage you' to fill in the gaps

see yourself as pawn or king, it is no matter
for at the end of every game, win or lose
you still call yourself a beautiful burning aftermaths of violence
wriggling into the body you designed yourself

# 6pm girl

walking barefoot on concrete floor and wearing bruise shade shorts
microscopic shards of last night embedded in skin
heart beating endlessly, heart breaking for an eternity
instructed as a burden but there's obligation and then creation
you'll find her in the 24 hour laundromat amongst faux silk pillows
    *and her stained glass kinda people?*

*you can smell the lavender in the daydreams the weaved just for her*

Mum and Dad, thank you for the hundreds of hours you both spent bored out your minds as I walked the shelves of bookshops. Thank you for every book you ever brought me. Lisa and Jacob, your support hasn't gone unnoticed either

I am deeply grateful for my friends whose collective excitement about seeing this collection finished stopped me from running away up some Welsh mountain to live as a hermit.

To all the strangers whose stories whispered softly in the background of my observations, thank you for unknowingly inspiring the words within these pages.

Arabella is a silent observer of the human experience, drawing inspiration from the everyday encounters and moments that often go unnoticed. When not lost in the world of writing, she can be found in a coffee shop or napping. Empty Vessels is her debut poetry collection, born from a desire to capture the essence of connection and curiosity in the spaces between us.


Barnard Publishing Ltd was established July 2022 and began trading that following November following the completion of Becca's Masters degree. Empty Vessels is their 9th publication